Sometimes My Mom Drinks Too Much

KIDS HAVE *TROUBLES* TOO

Sometimes My Mom Drinks Too Much

by Sheila Stewart and Rae Simons

Mason Crest Publishers

Copyright © 2011 by Mason Crest Publishers. All rights reserved. No part of this publication may be reproduced or transmitted in any form or by any means, electronic or mechanical, including photocopying, recording, taping, or any information storage and retrieval system, without permission from the publisher.

MASON CREST PUBLISHERS INC.
370 Reed Road
Broomall, Pennsylvania 19008
(866)MCP-BOOK (toll free)
www.masoncrest.com

First Printing
9 8 7 6 5 4 3 2 1

CIP data on file with the Library of Congress

ISBN (set) 978-1-4222-1691-0   ISBN 978-1-4222-1704-7
ISBN (ppbk set) 978-1-4222-1904-1   ISBN 978-1-4222-1917-1 (pbk.)

Design by MK Bassett-Harvey.
Produced by Harding House Publishing Service, Inc.
www.hardinghousepages.com
Cover design by Torque Advertising Design.
Printed in USA.

The creators of this book have made every effort to provide accurate information, but it should not be used as a substitute for the help and services of trained professionals.

Introduction

Each child is unique—and each child encounters a unique set of circumstances in life. Some of these circumstances are more challenging than others, and how a child copes with those challenges will depend in large part on the other resources in her life.

The issues children encounter cover a wide range. Some of these are common to almost all children, including threats to self-esteem, anger management, and learning to identify emotions. Others are more unique to individual families, but problems such as parental unemployment, a death in the family, or divorce and remarriage are common but traumatic events in many children's lives. Still others— like domestic abuse, alcoholism, and the incarceration of a family member—are unfortunately not uncommon in today's world.

Whatever problems a child encounters in life, understanding that he is not alone is a key component to helping him cope. These books, both their fiction and nonfiction elements, allow children to see that other children are in the same situations. The books make excellent tools for triggering conversation in a nonthreatening way. They will also promote understanding and compassion in children who may not be experiencing these issues themselves.

These books offer children important factual information—but perhaps more important, they offer hope.

—*Cindy Croft, M.A., Ed., Director of the Center for Inclusive Child Care*

Mom's car was in the driveway when I got off the school bus. No matter what else, she always made sure she was there when I got home. I wondered what she'd be doing when I got inside, though. I never knew what to expect.

Two days ago, I had come home and everything had been fine. Mom had been out earlier in the day taking pictures for a couple who had just had a baby and she was happy. We'd made spaghetti together and Dad had called that evening.

Yesterday, Mom had been a little quiet and sad when I got home from school. That made me nervous, but she was still okay. She helped me study for my social studies test after school and then later, after supper, she'd made popcorn and we watched TV for a while before bed. Then, right before bed, Mom had read me a chapter from *The Lord of the Rings*. I'm ten, but Mom says you're never too old for a bedtime story.

Everything was quiet when I walked in the door. I looked in the kitchen for Mom, but it was empty. Our cereal bowls and juice glasses from breakfast were still sitting on the table, which I didn't think was a good thing. I didn't see Mom in the living room either, so I went down the hall to her studio. The room was empty and the computer was off.

I was walking out of the studio when I heard a noise. I listened and heard it again. Click, click, click, click, click. I knew that sound. Somewhere in the house, Mom was taking pictures. She was always happier when she was taking pictures.

I followed the sound to Mom and Dad's room. The bed wasn't made and there was a pile of laundry in the corner. At first, I didn't see Mom, but then I saw the top of her head on the other side of the big bed. She was sitting on the floor, with her back against the bed, bent over looking at something in front of her. I walked around the bed to see what she was looking at.

Mom was leaning over, looking through the viewfinder of her camera at something on the floor. I couldn't see anything there, but she pushed the button again, and her camera whirred and clicked.

"Mom?" I wasn't sure what I should ask, or even if I should say anything. Sometimes I didn't know how she would react to even really normal questions.

Mom took her camera down from her face and looked up at me. "Sam," she said, and held out her hand to me.

I took a step closer to her and saw she had tears running down her face.

"He's almost dead," Mom said.

"Who is?" I asked, sitting down on the floor next to her. She put her arm around me and kissed the top of my head. I could smell the alcohol on her breath, which I'd known I would as soon as I'd seen she was crying. I looked past her and saw the bottle on the floor.

"The spider," Mom said. "I must have stepped on him without noticing. He's been trying to walk, trying to get home to his wife and babies, but he only has four legs now. He's not going to make it."

I looked more closely at the floor in front of her and saw the spider. It was moving just a little bit.

I hated it when Mom did this. She could be so much fun. She was funny and smart and inter-

esting and a much cooler mom than most of my friends had. But sometimes she started getting sad, and then she started drinking, and then she wasn't the same anymore. When Mom drank, anything could happen.

I picked up the poor spider with a tissue, took it down the hall to the bathroom, and flushed it down the toilet. I could hear her crying, and I wanted to go in my room and shut the door and put my head under my pillow. But I didn't. When Dad first got his job as an over-the-road trucker last year, he'd said that Mom and I would look after each other while he was gone. Mom said that parents always looked after kids, not the other way around, and that Dad had only meant I should help out around the house. But whenever Mom started drinking like this, I thought of what Dad had said.

"Come on, Mom," I said, going back into her bedroom. "Let's go out in the kitchen. Maybe I'll make some soup for supper."

Mom looked up at me and smiled, but it was such a sad smile that it made me want to cry too.

"You're a good boy, Sam," she said. "I love you so much. I'm not really hungry, though." She picked up the bottle from the floor beside her and took a tiny sip. She always drank alcohol in tiny sips like that—hundreds and hundreds of tiny sips.

I sat down beside her again, because I didn't know what else to do. We sat there for a really long time, until it started to get dark outside, and the bedroom got dark too. Mom kept taking tiny sips from the bottle, and I kept trying to think of what to do.

"Mom," I said finally, when it was too dark in the bedroom to see each other anymore, "we should go out in the living room. It's really dark in here."

"I don't mind the dark," she said. Her words were starting to slur together. "But I suppose you do. I remember when you were just a little baby you hated being in the dark."

"Come on." I stood up. "I'll help you up."

Mom took my hand, but I wasn't really strong enough to pull her up. It seemed like it took a really long time before she was finally on her feet.

We went out into the hall and I switched on the light. My eyes had gotten used to the dark, and the light made me blink.

"Do you want something to eat now?" I asked.

"No." Mom shook her head. "I think I just want to sit down again." She went into the living room and sat down on the couch, running into the armchair before she got there. She put the bottle down on the floor and covered her face with her hands.

I was starving—I hadn't eaten anything since lunch—but I couldn't stand seeing Mom like that. Instead of going to find some food, I sat down next to her and turned on the TV. I flicked through the channels, trying to find something that wouldn't make her cry anymore.

I stopped on a show of funny video clips. Everybody in the audience on the show kept laughing and laughing, like this was the best thing they'd ever seen, but when Mom finally looked up at the TV, she looked just as sad as ever.

The phone rang, and I switched off the TV before I got up to answer it.

"Hello?"

"Sam! My man! How are you doing?" It was Dad.

"I'm okay." I said. "How's it going?"

I never, ever told Dad about Mom drinking. For one thing, I liked to pretend it didn't really happen, especially when I was talking to Dad. I always acted as though everything was great, and sometimes it really was great. For another thing, though, I was afraid Dad would get mad at Mom. If he got mad at her for drinking, I was afraid she might drink even more. When she was really upset, sometimes she drank so much that she just fell asleep. I really worried about her then.

"I'm doing just fine," Dad said, on the phone. "I've been hauling a load over the mountains. It's so beautiful here."

"Is that your dad?" Mom asked from behind me, and I nodded at her.

She put out her hand to take the phone. I didn't want to give it to her, because I didn't want Dad to realize she had been drinking. She kept holding out her hand, though, so I told Dad Mom wanted to talk to him, and then I gave her the phone.

"Will!" Mom said into the phone, sounding so happy to hear Dad's voice.

I didn't want to listen to Mom on the phone, so I went to the kitchen and made myself a sandwich. I tried to do my homework while I ate the sandwich, but it was hard to concentrate. Mom's voice from the living room started getting louder.

"But I need you to come home, Will! Sam needs you and I need you. We aren't okay without you. And not just for a weekend or a week, either. We need you here to stay!"

I left my food on the kitchen table and went back to the living room. Mom had started sobbing.

"I will not calm down!" she yelled. "I don't care about the money! We can go live in a box and I won't care! As long as you're there too!" And then she slammed the phone down.

I waited for the phone to ring again, for Dad to call back, but nothing happened. Thanks a lot, Dad, I thought.

Mom was still standing by the phone sobbing. Suddenly, she screamed, picked up a glass dish that was sitting on the little table next to her, and threw it across the room. Then she picked up the bottle from the floor and drank the rest of it all at once. She kind of fell over onto the couch then. I could still hear her crying, though, so I knew she wasn't dead.

I sat down on the floor in the hall, put my head on my knees and my arms over my head. I wished I knew what to do.

Eventually, Mom fell asleep. I could hear her snoring just a little bit. I went over and looked at her. Her face was puffy and wet from crying. I took a blanket off the back of the couch and covered her up.

After that, I went to bed. There didn't seem to be anything else to do. I could have finished my homework, I guess, but I couldn't even try to think about homework. I lay in bed, and I couldn't sleep at all. All I could think about was Mom, and I started crying. I didn't know what to do to help her and no matter what I did, she seemed to get a little worse all the time. She'd be like this for a few days and then she'd be okay for a little while, but then it would get bad again. The bad times were starting to get worse, though, and the good times didn't seem to last as long. I knew Mom was upset that Dad was away so much, but I was really, really worried that maybe I was doing something to make it worse for her.

The next morning, Mom was still asleep on the couch, looking a little more peaceful. My half-eaten sandwich was on the table where I had left it, along with the homework I had barely even started. I stuck the sandwich in a bag for my lunch, threw everything in my backpack, and ran out the door to catch the bus.

All day at school, I worried about Mom. I got yelled at three times to pay attention and had to stay inside at recess to finish the homework I hadn't done the night before.

I wondered if people could drink so much alcohol that they stayed asleep forever, like being in a coma.

By the time I got off the bus after school, I was so worried I thought I might throw up. As soon as I opened the door, though, I heard music, which meant that Mom wasn't still asleep at least. I also smelled something really delicious.

"Sam?" Mom called from the kitchen, and then came over to the door where I was taking off my sneakers.

She hugged me, and I hugged her back, but I could still smell alcohol, so I couldn't relax and be happy. She looked a lot happier, though.

"I have a surprise," Mom said. "I think that yesterday was a bad day, and I'm sorry about that. It's not your fault and you shouldn't have to deal with it." She stopped and took a deep breath. "Come here," she said, pulling me into the kitchen.

On the kitchen table was a tray of cupcakes. Mom had decorated them with blue frosting and red and yellow swirls of sprinkles. Two of the cupcakes each had a candle in it. I frowned at the cupcakes.

"Surprise! Happy Birthday!" Mom said.

"But it's not my birthday," I said. My birthday wasn't for another four months, and Mom's was the month after that.

"Well, no," Mom said. "That's the surprise part."

I laughed. This was something Mom would do when she was okay, so I thought maybe things were better after all.

"I'll light the candles," Mom said. "Then we'll each get to make a wish and blow out our candle."

She went over to the drawer where the matches were, but stopped first to take a drink from the bottle on the counter. I stopped feeling better as soon as I saw the bottle.

"Okay," Mom said. She took out a match and struck it against the box, but then something happened. She must not have been holding the match well enough, because, even though it lit, it went flying out of her fingers and onto the box of tissues on the counter. The tissues started burning, and the flames jumped up way above the box.

"Oh no!" Mom's face scrunched up as she started to cry.

"Mom!" I yelled. "Do something! Put it out!"

But she didn't do anything except stare at the fire and cry.

I was scared. My grandfather's house burned down when I was little, and I've always had nightmares about my house catching on fire.

In the sink was the mixing bowl Mom had used when she made the cupcakes, with a wooden spoon next to it. I grabbed the spoon and pushed the burning box of tissues into the sink. Then I turned on the faucet and splashed water onto the fire.

When the fire was out, I realized that the kitchen was full of smoke, and the smoke alarm was beeping. The half-burned tissue box was a soggy mess in the sink.

I looked at Mom. She had stopped crying and was staring at the counter where the fire had been a couple of seconds before.

"Oh Sam," she whispered. "I'm so sorry."

"It's okay." I didn't know what else to say.

"No, it's not okay," she said. "You're not okay. I'm not okay. What I'm doing is not okay. I have to stop drinking. Somehow. I've tried before. I didn't tell anyone I was trying, but I did try. It just didn't work." She grabbed me and hugged me. "I could have killed you, Sam. I could have burned the whole house down. I'm kind of drunk even now. I wish I wasn't."

I still didn't know what to say, but I didn't tell her it was okay again. She was right, it wasn't okay.

"I'm telling you this because someone else needs to know. I need other people to help me do this. It's not your job, but you need to know I'm going to try. I have a phone number in my studio that I picked up in the waiting room at the doctor's office. A brochure about alcoholism. I don't know if I should call when I've been drinking, but I'm afraid I won't call if I don't do it right now." She hugged me tighter for a minute and took a big breath, like a gasp.

"This is what we're going to do," she said. "We're going to go to my studio and I'm going to call that number. Then we're going to call your Dad. He needs to know what's going on."

Mom let go of me enough so we could walk down the hall to her studio. She opened a drawer in her desk and flipped through the files, finally pulling out a brochure that had been folded in half and stuck in the back behind all the files.

She put the brochure down on the desk and we both stared at it. I wasn't sure what I was thinking. I didn't know if I should even hope anymore that things would get better, but Mom could be so great—when she wasn't drinking—that I wanted to hope. I wanted her to be that way all the time.

Mom picked up the phone on her desk and looked at me. Then she dialed the phone.

Alcoholism

Sam's mom has what is called alcoholism. She is addicted to drinking alcohol, which means that her body and brain need it to feel good, so she keeps drinking it. Alcoholism messes up people's lives—not only the life of the person who's drinking, but the lives of her friends and family too.

Understand the Word

Genetics has to do with how biological traits are passed down through generations. You might have inherited your mom's red hair or your dad's eyes, which is because you have their genes.

Alcoholism is a disease, not a failure on the part of the alcoholic. Doctors are still studying it, but it might have something to do with **genetics**. Some people are just more likely to become alcoholics than others, especially if something triggers it. In Sam's case, his mom was upset that his father was away all the time, and she turned to alcohol to make herself feel better. What actually happened was that drinking made her feel worse, and it made Sam worried and sad.

Adults can drink but not be alcoholics. Drinking a beer or some wine with dinner is not the same thing as alcoholism. Adults usually know how to drink alcohol responsibly, and do it socially, with other people.

Alcoholics don't just drink a glass of wine at dinner. They drink too much, too often, and sometimes drink alone.

Alcoholics drink all the time, though, and they often do it while they're by themselves. They can't control their craving for alcohol, and it gets in the way of them being able to live their lives normally. The vast majority of adults who drink are not alcoholics, but there are some people who abuse alcohol and become addicted.

Without help, alcoholics are in trouble. Alcohol poisoning happens when someone drinks too much, and that can cause coma and death. Even if an alcoholic doesn't poison himself, he still may not be able to hold a job, have good relationships, or be happy. Like Sam's mom, alcoholics aren't in control of their actions and movements, and they can put other people in danger too. Whether it's the inability to light a match, or driving drunk, alcoholics can hurt or kill other people.

Kids and Alcoholism

You aren't alone if one of your parents is an alcoholic. About 6.6 million kids live with an alcoholic parent. That's a lot of kids who have to deal with the problems that alcohol causes at home. Parents have certain responsibilities toward their kids, and when they are drunk or **hung over**, or depressed, they can't follow through on those responsibilities.

Too Many Feelings

Kids respond to alcoholism at home in many ways. If your parent is an alcoholic you could feel sad, angry, guilty, lonely, embarrassed, or confused. In the story, Sam was mostly sad and worried. He loved his mom, and he wanted to help her, but he didn't know how. That's a common response to an alcoholic parent. You're just a kid, after all—how are you supposed to solve such a big, grownup problem like alcohol addiction?

Some kids get angry at their alcoholic parent, or at the world. They don't understand how their mom or dad could be so messed up and so **neglectful**. If you feel angry, that's normal. It's completely okay to be angry, but don't take it out on other people. Take out your anger and aggression during soccer practice, dance to loud

Understand the Word

Hung over is how you feel after you've been drunk on too many drinks. After the effects of alcohol wear off, a person suffers from tiredness, headaches, nausea, and sensitivity to light.

Someone is **neglectful** if they don't pay attention to something the way they should. In this case, a parent can be neglectful of children if he or she doesn't feed them, keep them clean, or give them love.

If your parent is an alcoholic, it's natural to feel angry, sad, frustrated, scared, or a mixture of all of them.

music, or take deep breaths to calm yourself down. Don't yell at other people or to turn to violence to let out your anger.

Sometimes the child of an alcoholic parent feels guilty, thinking that he caused their parent's problem. However, it's always the parent's problem, never the kid's. Even if you feel bad about something you did to make your mom angry or to annoy her, think of all the ways she could have dealt with it that didn't include drinking. Alcoholism is an individual, personal problem, not one caused by other people.

Lots of kids feel ashamed or embarrassed about having an alcoholic parent. They don't want to tell their friends that their mom or dad has a drinking problem, so they keep it a secret. They think that other people will make fun of them, but that's probably not true. If you decide to tell people you trust about your parent's problem, they will instead likely be **supportive** and **sympathetic**, or they might not really understand what you're talking about until you explain it to them.

Understand the Word

You are **supportive** and **sympathetic** when you show another person that you understand that they're going through a rough time and that you want to help them any way you can. Being supportive and sympathetic involves being kind and not judging the person for her problems.

Why You Feel This Way

Alcoholism causes a lot of unpleasant changes at home. Sam had to worry about what mood his mom was in when he got home, he was afraid to ask his mom questions, and he had to stay with his mom to make sure she was okay while she was drinking. Kids have to be sensitive to their parent's changing moods, and they have to stay on their toes to deal with their unpredictable behavior.

Sam, and other kids like him, often feel completely alone and helpless. They don't know where to turn or how to get their parent and themselves help. It's hard to talk to the parents about it, because they might deny it or get angry or sad. At the same time, kids often don't want to make the situation worse by getting someone else involved. It's a big issue for a kid to deal with, and it can cause all sorts of reactions.

When a Kid Has to Be the Parent

Having an alcoholic parent can get in the way of having a normal childhood. Instead of playing with your

Kids with alcoholic parents sometimes have to do more grown-up things like laundry, cooking, or taking care of little brothers and sisters.

friends, coming home to a homemade meal, and getting tucked into bed, you might have to make dinner yourself or take care of younger siblings. Sam had to go without supper until he made a sandwich, and he had to put out the fire in his house himself.

Parents who are under the influence of alcohol can't always take care of themselves, let alone their children. Their sons and daughters have to take more responsibility and act more like adults than kids or

Alcoholism gets in the way of having a normal, happy home life.

teenagers. Having time to explore the world and learn from parents is part of what childhood is all about, and if your mom or dad isn't there to help you do that, then you're not getting that childhood. That's just one reason why alcoholic parents need to get help. You deserve to have a chance to be a kid!

Lashing Out

Some kids become more responsible, almost like mini-adults, but others turn into troublemakers. All that confusion at home makes them want to lash out and take control of things by causing trouble. Also, alcoholic parents don't always pay that much attention to their kids. If you're not getting attention and love at home, then you might decide to force attention on yourself. Starting fights, pulling pranks, and staying out late past your bedtime will definitely get you attention at school and at home. Unfortunately, it's not really the attention you want, and you could end up grounded, suspended, and disliked by your friends. Instead of making trouble, you should get attention in positive ways, by doing well at sports, art, or

In order to get more attention, you might want to start causing trouble.
This will just put you in detention, get you grounded, or worse.

schoolwork, or by talking to trusted adults who will listen to your problems.

What Should You Do?

It's hard to know what to do in a situation like this. Fortunately, there is a lot of help out there, if you know where to look. You don't even have to confront your mom and dad directly, if you can't bring yourself to talk about it with them, or if you think it will make them upset. Instead, talk to a teacher, a family friend, a coach, or a religious leader. Some schools have D.A.R.E. (Drug and Alcohol Resistance Education) officers, who can talk to you specifically about alcohol-related things.

Better yet, set up an appointment with your school counselor. Most schools have a counselor whose job it is to talk to students. They listen to their problems, whether it's problems with friends, with doing well in school, or serious things like parents' alcoholism, and then they help you find ways to deal with those problems. Talk to a teacher or other adult at school to help you set up an appointment with a counselor, if you don't already know how to do it.

If you want to talk to someone completely **anonymously**, then consider calling an organization with a hotline. Al-Anon/Alateen has a 24-hour hotline you can call at 1-800-344-2666, where you can talk to someone you don't know about your problems. They won't ask who you are, and they won't track you down, so you can feel free to say anything you want.

There are also support groups around, filled with kids just like you. Support groups are meetings of people who all have the same issues, and can compare how they feel and how they're dealing. Alateen, the same organization with the hotline, also has support groups for young people who are dealing with alcoholics at home. Alcoholics Anonymous also has services for people living with alcoholics.

How to Get Your Parent Help

Sam was lucky: his mom decided that her alcoholism was bad, and she needed some help. He didn't have to convince her to call someone or go to the doctor, which can be very difficult to do.

It takes courage to call someone to help you out if you have an alcoholic parent, but you'll feel better once you talk about your problem.

It's hard for adults to make alcoholics get help, and it's even harder for kids. The best thing to do would be to let an adult handle it. If no one knows your mom is an alcoholic, then you should tell someone so your parent can get the help she needs. Let another adult figure out how to get your parent to decide to stop drinking. A family friend, an aunt or an uncle, or

Alcoholism is a serious disease; alcoholics should get help as soon as possible.

a grandparent might convince your parent to call Alcoholics Anonymous, go see a doctor, or even enter rehab. Rehab is a place where alcoholics and other drug abusers go to live for a while, so that they can get over their addiction. Your parent will be gone for a little while if he starts rehab, but when he comes back, he will be better able to fight his alcoholism. He will hopefully be more like he was before he started drinking.

After Alcoholism

Even if your mom or dad is an alcoholic, you still love them. Maybe you can remember a time when your dad wasn't drinking constantly, or all those times your mom took care of you when you were sick. They're still your parents, even if it doesn't always seem like it.

If your parent gets help, then she can get better. You can be part of that process, and let her know how much you support and love her. If she knows she has someone who is behind her one-hundred percent, then she has a better chance of beating her alcoholism and being a true parent again.

Questions to Think About

1. What do you think will happen next in Sam's life? Do you think his life will get better right away? Why or why not?

2. How do you feel about Sam's mother? Do you feel like she's a nice person? Or do you feel angry with her? Why?

3. What about Sam's dad? What do you think he will say and do when he finds out his wife has such a serious problem?

4. If you were Sam's friend, what would you say to him?

Further Reading

Black, Claudia. *My Dad Loves Me, My Dad Has a Disease: A Child's View: Living with Addiction.* Bainbridge Island, Wash.: MAC Publishing, 1997.

Hastings, Jill M. and Marion H. Typpo. *An Elephant in the Living Room: The Children's Book.* Center City, Minn.: Hazelden, 1984.

Seixas, Judith A. and Geraldine Youcha. *Children of Alcoholism: A Survivor's Manual.* New York: Crown Publishers, 1985.

Find Out More on the Internet

Al-Anon/Alateen
www.al-anon.alateen.org/alateen.html

National Association for Children of Alcoholics
www.nacoa.org

The websites listed on this page were active at the time of publication. The publisher is not responsible for websites that have changed their address or discontinued operation since the date of publication. The publisher will review and update the websites upon each reprint.

Index

Picture Credits

About the Authors

Sheila Stewart has written several dozen books for young people, both fiction and nonfiction, although she especially enjoys writing fiction. She has a master's degree in English and now works as a writer and editor. She lives with her two children in a house overflowing with books, in the Southern Tier of New York State.

Rae Simons is a freelance author who has written numerous educational books for children and young adults. She also has degrees in psychology and special education, and she has worked with children encountering a range of troubles in their lives.

About the Consultant

Cindy Croft, M.A. Ed., is Director of the Center for Inclusive Child Care, a state-funded program with support from the McKnight Foundation, that creates, promotes, and supports pathways to successful inclusive care for all children. Its goal is inclusion and retention of children with disabilities and behavioral challenges in community child care settings. Cindy Croft is also on the faculty at Concordia University, where she teaches courses on young children with special needs and the emotional growth of young children. She is the author of several books, including *The Six Keys: Strategies for Promoting Children's Mental Health*.